TRAUMA FOCUSED CBT FOR CHILDREN AND ADOLESCENTS: THE PRACTICAL GUIDE FOR HEALING DEVELOPMENTAL TRAUMA AND COMING OUT OF PTSD

Zecaina N.N.

I would like to dedicate this book to everyone out there that is struggling with the monster of development trauma. This book is a reminder that you're not alone as you are fighting to win the mental war.

"Just as pain is a way of your body telling you something is awfully wrong, trauma is how your subconscious mind tells you everything isn't okay upstairs. Unfortunately, the human brain is very complicated, and mostly, we end up acting inappropriately to messages it gives us as a result of misinterpretation."

CHRIS

CONTENTS

PREFACE

This book was written to create awareness and increase knowledge of the developmental trauma disorder. It seeks to provide a way out from the ghosts that persistently haunt the minds of the traumatized.

CHAPTER 1: BACKGROUND INFORMATION ON THE DEVELOPMENTAL TRAUMA DISORDER

Development Trauma is a less known variation of Post-Traumatic Stress Disorder, but both medical conditions have the same level of adverse effects. Unlike Post Traumatic Stress Disorder which is mostly experienced by individuals who are exposed to extremely violent occurrences, Developmental Trauma Disorder is experienced by individuals who grow under impoverished, unstable, and abusive conditions. Thus, this health condition is highly prevalent in minors. It is often caused by experiencing of physical or sexual abuse, substance abuse, parental absence, psychological issues, or emotional neglect. However, one of the most considerable cause of Developmental Trauma Disorder is sexual abuse since approximately 4.2 million individuals in the US alone have been sexually victimized at one point or another in their entire lives. Developmental Trauma Disorder is not accorded sufficient attention, even though it consequently leads to educational attainment issues, sexually risky tendencies, and criminal behavior.

CHAPTER 2: THE PSYCHOLOGICAL EFFECTS OF THE DEVELOPMENTAL TRAUMA DISORDER

1. Low Self-Esteem

The sense of self-worth and self-value in an individual is often determined by the manner in which they are treated by the people that are closest to them from birth. Thus, when a primary caregiver subjects a minor to neglect or abuse, the child is highly likely to internalize the message that they are not worthy, valuable, and loveable. This phenomenon is referred to as attachment trauma within the field of psychology.

One significant form of negligent caregiving is parentification, which involves the primary caregiver putting considerably intensive and extensive responsibilities on the child. This practice can manifest through actions such as caregivers relying on children for their emotional and physical needs. Parentification often leads to the child learning that their needs are less significant. In the later stages of life, such children are likely to develop a behavioral pattern referred to as "people pleaser" that implies an individual who is afraid of setting boundaries in relationships and saying no.

However, it should be noted that negligent and abusive caregivers are not the only causes of this psychological state as some loving parents that lack empathetic skills required by children might unintentionally cause the same effect.

2. Harsh Self-Criticism

Once a minor internalizes the message that they are not worthy, valuable, and loveable, they often nurture a belief that they have some form of imperfections, and thus, they are somehow not good enough. This process consequently leads to self-blame in that the child feels they are to blame for the form of treatment they received from their primary caregiver. They end up thinking that maybe if they had been better, their parents or guardians would have loved or cared for them more. This psychological state can particularly cause children to be harder on themselves that most ordinary people would. And, this self-judgement often occurs automatically without the minor noticing since it happens subconsciously.

There is reason to believe that the behavioral pattern of harsh self-judgement occurs as a result of primary caregivers denying children the space to express negative and confused emotions such as anger. When this situation occurs, the children are forced to internalize their emotions as a coping mechanism for survival. As a result, children exposed to attachment trauma and internalized emotions tends to exhibit self-criticism, shame, and guilt; and low self-esteem, as mentioned earlier.

3. Display An Excessive Temper

When an individual feels unimportant or worthless, vulnerable, and ignored or rejected, they might utilize anger as a mask to counteract the previously mentioned emotions. They may also get angry to get control over experiences that triggered the emotions in question.

In order to understand how anger relates to development trauma, it is fundamental to understand the physiology of anger. Scientists have determined that when an individual becomes angry, there is a chemical reaction that occurs throughout the body. The brain often secretes a hormone that is referred to as norepinephrine, which is more of an analgesic / painkiller as it numbs emotional pain. The brain further releases another hormone called epinephrine that causes an immediate spike in energy levels thus making an individual feel more invincible and powerful.

Feeling a numbing of emotional pain and increased power or invincibility can make a person that was previously experiencing feelings of being unimportant or worthless, vulnerable, and ignored or rejected, as a result of development trauma, to start feeling in command and in control or dominant. Thus, anger can be a defense mechanism that brings about instant relief for some of the subsequent emotions of attachment trauma. Therefore, it's not uncommon for people to become addicted to the chemical reactions caused by the epinephrine and norepinephrine hormones just as they would get used drugs. This causes an individual to lose their anger often, and in the event, they don't realize that externalization of their anger has a negative impact on the recipient.

Destructive anger often manifests in two primary ways - passive aggression and open aggression. The first form of anger is often adopted by individuals that do not like being involved in a confrontation, and thus, when involved in such situations they avoid expressing their anger directly. Such individuals choose to either openly claim that all is okay and they are not angry yet they are harboring feelings of rage or become sulky and defensive or silent. Passive aggressive individuals will often externalize their anger through actions such as cynicism and veiled hostility.

The second form of anger projection, open aggression, is adopted by individuals that do not mind being involved in confrontations. Such people often escalate confrontations by being verbally abusive in that they accuse and shout at the other party while being sarcastic and mean. If their anger does not subside after the outburst, they might escalate the situation by opting for physical violence.

4. Learning Disabilities

First, Developmental Trauma Disorder undermines

cognitive processes that are fundamental for learning, and thus, necessary in order for one to be academically prosperous. The cognitive processes in question are majorly two - critical thinking and problem solving, which are mental processes that have to be nurtured and enhanced by an individual before learning can effectively occur. However, once a person, more so a child, has been exposed to a traumatic experience, they might have challenges in terms of reasoning logically and thinking clearly, which is considered vital for optimal cognitive capacity. Therefore, a major proportion of children suffering from the psychological condition are severely incapacitated in terms of anticipating the future by planning ahead and acting accordingly, and acquiring of new skills and knowledge.

This is principally because children who are exposed to traumatic events during the early stages of development usually focus most of their psychological and physiological resources towards survival. Constant and regular exposure to occurrences that are traumatic enhance perception of danger and adversity by minors. Once this occurs, they tend to establish and develop their survival instincts. Therefore, even when there are no signs of adversity, the traumatized mind of a child will not process this information and act accordingly. This consequently leads to the child being distracted from competently taking in novel information while undergoing the learning process.

Also, when a minor is subjected to consistent and continuous trauma in the form of negligence and abuse, more so at extensive and extreme levels, they learn that responding through anger externalization can cause them to experience more pain from their caregivers. This consequently motivates them to internalize their anger rather than expressing it as they feel powerless against their adult caregivers that are causing the trauma. The process of anger internalization can necessitate emotional distress levels that limit the ability of an individual to cope as it reaches intolerable levels. Conversely, the nervous system of a human being is designed to protect itself in the face of intensive and extensive emotional distress. Thus, intolerable levels of this distress can lead to a process otherwise referred to as dissociation whereby the nervous system regulates itself downwards to subsequently shut off all the painful emotions.

In more layman terms, dissociation is known as being on autopilot or zoning out, and it often causes a sense of numbness. If it occurs severally in a child, it can lead to a disconnection between thoughts, feeling, behavior, and sense of oneself. Thus, chronic dissociation can make it challenging for an individual to focus yet this phenomenon is fundamental in the process of learning. This particularly implies that a child with an issue of chronic dissociation as a result of development trauma tends to develop learning disabilities. Statistical data can support this argument since averagely 25% of children who are exposed to sexual or physical abuse usually end up dropping out of formal education while at the secondary level of learning. There is a direct and irrefutable link between childhood trauma and learning challenges.

5. Distrust And Insecurity

The first connection created after birth with the primary caregiver often determines how an individual is going to interact with other people and form relationships throughout their lives. Hence, a confusing, traumatic, stressful relationship between a child and their caregiver, which borders on shame, fear, and unreliability can be translated into all future relationships such as work connections, friendships, and romantic relationships. Such kind of relationships are referred to as disrupted bonds between children and their caregivers, and have often been associated with insecure attachment.

Based on the information provided above, it is common for individuals exposed to development trauma, otherwise referred to as a primal wound, to find it challenging to trust anyone. Thus, they often limit the process of sharing their inner true selves and their actual emotions. This type of coping behavior is called insecure avoidant whereby the individual tries, by all means possible, to avoid being reliant on others due to the fact that they fear rejection or betrayal.

6. Need For Attention And Reassurance

In case of trust occurring in subsequent relationships after attachment trauma, it often manifests on the form of insecurity. This implies that the traumatized individual will tend to be clingy and needy in all relationships. This can be evidenced through the constant need for assurance that they are loved.

7. Inability To Maintain Relationships

As a result of the distrust and insecurity issues mentioned above, a child exposed to development trauma might find it challenging in regards to creating different types of relationships. This is because they don't want to like another person and get comfortable around them thus letting their guard down, which could lead to betrayal or rejection. Chronic dissociation can also cause socialization challenges in the later stages of life as an individual finds it difficult to maintain healthy relationships. Besides, the anger management issues that occur as a result of development trauma, as discussed previously, can make it difficult for individuals to maintain healthy relationships since their rage outbursts create conflict.

7. Sexually Risky Behavior

Additionally, children who are exposed to traumatic experiences in their early stages of growth and development tend to portray behavior that is considered sexually risky in their subsequent stages of life. For this effect of childhood trauma to be understood, it is imperative that it be analyzed from the perspective of Helena Evans, a female that is 56 years old. Evans was a sexual worker for a period of close to three decades, and it all started when she was just 13 years old. She was majorly motivated to become a sexual worker because she had been severely defiled in her life, with her first experience happening when she was 12 years old. According to her, engaging in sexual acts in exchange for financial rewards made her feel worthy and in control of her life. Contrarily, defilement enhanced her self-conception as a worthless human being. Therefore, she opted to become a sexual worker rather than be incorporated into a child homecare system where she was abused sexually on several instances.

Most minors who are exposed to sexual abuse, more so females, have a significantly higher probability of portraying risky sexual behavior. This particular traumatic event subsequently causes early and non-marital childbearing in females during the later stages of their lives. Female individuals who were defiled during the early stages of life are more likely to bear their first child before 25 years of age, more so during adolescence. Almost half of the women who had teenage pregnancies have a history of sexual abuse. Most of these pregnancies are usually unintended. However, unintended pregnancies are not the only negative effects that could occur from risky sexual tendencies. This particular behavior could also result in health issues which are sexually transmitted.

8. Criminal Behavioral Patterns

Finally, exposure of minors to traumatizing events in the early stages of growth and development consequently increases the likelihood of them portraying criminal behavior and socially deviant tendencies. Most of the individuals incorporated into the criminal justice system and incarcerated in Correctional Service facilities experienced childhood trauma at one point in the course of their lives. Therefore, this implies that most of the burglars, robbers, psychopath serial killers, and homicidal individuals in various societal and communal contexts were influenced into these violent tendencies by the occurrence of traumatic events in their childhood. As much as other factors and determinants also influence the criminal behaviors and tendencies in society, childhood trauma plays a significant contributing part that cannot be assumed. Failure to competently deal with and manage Developmental Trauma Disorder subsequently results in flourishing and thriving of crime globally.

Over 75% of the children who are incorporated into the juvenile justice system per year report to have been exposed to some form of trauma. On the other hand, female individuals in the adult Correctional Service system are twice more likely to have been sexually or physically abused in the early stages of their lives. The individuals mentioned above portrayed delinquency duly because they have established and developed a self-conception of being social misfits who are maleficent. This particular self-conception is nurtured and enhanced by occurrence of events that exposed them to exploitation and abuse. Once this perception has been reinforced, an individual has a tendency of engaging in socially disapproved activities.

Overall, it is evident that once exposed to traumatizing events in the early stages of life, the brains of minors are not sufficiently capable of processing the occurrences in a mentally mature manner like adults. Trauma modifies the psychological and physiological functionality of a child which in turn affects the growth and development process. Children usually cannot manage to regain a sense of normalcy once they have experienced traumatizing occurrences. This consequently leads to issues in the later stages of their lives. For instance, childhood traumatization usually leads to portraying of criminal behavior and socially deviant tendencies; experiencing cognitive and learning challenges which undermines educational success; having sexually risky behavior; and maladaptive coping skills like chronic dissociation, anger management issues, distrust and insecurity issues, low self-esteem, self-criticism, and regressive behavioral patterns.

CHAPTER 3: IMPACT OF UNHELPFUL THINKING ON THE DEVELOPMENTAL TRAUMA DISORDER

Some of the signs and symptoms of development trauma, which are discussed above, are motivated or rather caused by unhelpful thinking or negative automatic thoughts. Such kind of cognitive patterns intrude on your mind without you necessarily making any effort to have them. From a superficial perspective, unhelpful thinking or negative automatic thoughts seems pretty believable, and thus, they tend to cause an upset to the emotions of an individual experiencing them, and the subsequent behavioral patterns. Psychologists have determined that there can be different forms of unhelpful thinking or negative automatic thoughts. Some of them are mentioned below to allow for the development of a connection to the signs and symptoms of development trauma.

1. Catastrophising

Some individuals who have experienced attachment trauma tends to develop a consistent expectation of the worst happening regardless of the situation they are involved in. This consequently causes excessive fear that they will not be able to cope with the situation once something terrible happens. Thus, such individuals always end up trying to prepare for the worst case scenario all the time.

This can be exhibited through behavioral patterns such as distrust and insecurity. A traumatized individual with the catastrophising pattern of cognition tends to think that everybody is out to cause physical or psychological harm to them, and thus, they do not let their guard down and get comfortable around anyone easily.

Also, catastrophising can consequently lead to anger management issues. This is mainly due to the fact that excessive fear and worry about the worst case scenario happening causes one to divert a lot energy and time towards these emotions. Thus, if something terrible happens, the individual finds it challenging to cope since they are already exhausted from worrying. The entire process mentioned above can lead to the manifestation of anger and frustration after failing to cope with the terrible occurrences.

2. Jumping To Conclusions

Also, individuals exposed to development trauma often exhibit the cognitive pattern of jumping to conclusions, which is also a form of unhelpful thinking. People that often jump into conclusions find themselves thinking that they are aware why someone undertook certain actions or a certain event occurred. This process occurs despite the lack of sufficient evidence to support the conclusions arrived at. If the process of jumping into conclusions finds fault in oneself, it might lead to low self-esteem / self-criticism. Conversely, if the same process finds fault in another party, it results in anger and distrust or insecurity.

3. Mind Reading

Most people tend to make assumptions in regards to what others might be thinking within a certain situation. This is because they assume they are effective in regards to reading the minds of others. But, these assumptions are always far from the truth, and in most instances, they are negative for individuals with development trauma. The consequences of trying to mind read someone can be extensive. Case in point, if you think someone is seeing you as worthless and unlovable, you are likely to have low self-esteem / self-criticism. Also, if you feel someone has wronged you, and you end up thinking they did it intentionally, or they are not apologetic, you most probably will become angry. Last, if you think someone doesn't have good intentions towards you, you will end up becoming distrustful or insecure around them.

4. Focusing On The Negatives

Besides, psychological evidence suggests that a significant proportion of human beings often disregard the positive elements of life, situations, or relationships and focus extensively on the negative aspects. When it occurs in individuals with development trauma, it can consequently increase expression of some of the signs and symptoms. Case in point, you might succeed in a lot of things in your life but end up thinking about that one time you failed thus end up perceiving yourself as a failure, which causes low self-esteem / self-criticism. Besides, someone might do a lot of good things for you but when they mess up at one point, you end up remembering the wrongs they did rather than the good actions which leads to anger. Finally, you might meet a lot of people that actually care about you and love you, but end up thinking about that one person that betrayed or hurt you hence being distrustful or insecure around people.

5. Black And White Thinking

People are more likely to perceive life and situations as either right or wrong and good or bad with no in between or rather gray area. This leaves no room for rationalizing the occurrence of mistakes or wrongs. And thus, one can't be understanding when something bad happens. Such kind of unhelpful thinking can result in low self-esteem / self-criticism if fault is found in oneself or anger and distrust or insecurity if someone else is to blame.

6. Must And Should Statements

There is reason to believe that a significant proportion of human beings often internalize some specific and fixed rules about how they or other people should conduct themselves under normal circumstances. This rules are what can be referred to as must and should statements, and once they are not met, harsh judgement is most likely to occur. Such kind of unhelpful thinking can result in low self-esteem / self-criticism if fault is found in oneself or anger and distrust or insecurity if someone else is to blame.

7. Taking Things Personally

Individuals with development trauma, as previously mentioned, tend to exhibit low self-esteem / self-criticism, anger, and distrust or insecurity. Thus, they often are highly sensitive to life occurrences and situations. This implies that they are highly likely to read too much into what others say or do.

CHAPTER 4:

CONTROLLING THE SYMPTOMS OF THE DEVELOPMENTAL TRAUMA DISORDER

In order for one to treat the signs and symptoms of development trauma, and enable recovery, they must be able to identify the unhelpful thinking or negative automatic thoughts behind some of their behavioral patterns (low self-esteem / self-criticism, anger, and distrust or insecurity). In order to achieve this process, you need to create a workbook centered on development trauma. This workbook is often divided into two major sections whereby the first section is aimed at identifying unhelpful thinking or negative automatic thoughts and the second section endeavors to find a solution to these cognitive patterns thus managing and controlling the subsequent behavioral patterns (low self-esteem / self-criticism, anger, and distrust or insecurity).

1. Guideline Of The First Section Of The Workbook

Situation or experience: What happened to you? Where were you at that moment? and Who were you with?

Feelings: What are the emotions that you experienced or rather felt?

Behavioral patterns: What actions did you undertake as a result of the emotions mentioned above?

Unhelpful thinking or negative automatic thoughts: What thoughts do you have as the situation occurred? What form of unhelpful thinking or negative automatic thoughts did you have?

You should fill the first section of the workbook, which is presented above, for a period of around 1 to 2 weeks. Any moment you experience low self-esteem / self-criticism, anger, and distrust or insecurity, you should proceed to fill in the questions provided. Afterwards, you should proceed to fill the questions for section two.

2. Guideline Of The Second Section Of The Workbook:

1. What patterns of unhelpful thinking or negative automatic thoughts have you identified a d pinpointed from the first section of the workbook?

In order to answer this particular question, you should use the answers you provided in the first section of the workbook.

2. What evidence can you provide to support or argue against the unhelpful thinking or negative automatic thoughts?

For example, you might think the way someone looks at you is evidence they're thinking negatively about you.

The evidence against a thought like that is you can never really tell what another person is thinking unless they tell you.

3. Based on the evidence you have generated in the preceding section; do you believe the unhelpful thinking or negative automatic thoughts are a fact or opinion?

A fact should be highly based on reality, and in order to determine this, you should consider whether the evidence is true, it cannot be disproved, and it is based on rationality.

An opinion, on the other hand, should be centered on personal beliefs, it can be argued against, it can be altered, and it is caused and motivated by emotions.

4. If your friend was in a situation similar to yours and had the same unhelpful thinking or negative automatic thoughts, what would you tell them?

Psychologists have determined that most individuals tend to be less harsh or kinder to their friends as compared to how they would be to themselves. Thus, you should think of the most appropriate advice you would give to a friend experiencing a situation similar to yours and take this advice yourself.

5. Is there another method that you can utilize and apply to handle and deal with the situation with a more beneficial outcome?

In order to effectively answer this particular question, you should adopt the perspective of an outside perspective in regards to the situation that caused unhelpful thinking or negative automatic thoughts. Consequently, determine how a person with an outside perspective would perceive the entire situation. Also, consider the same situation from the point of the other people involved directly in your experience with you, and try to determine what would be their thoughts and feelings regarding this situation. You should be informed that this is adopting the point of view of another person and not mind reading or making assumptions.

6. Question yourself about why you are having low self-esteem / self-criticism, anger, or distrust and insecurity, and what you are reacting to when you exhibit these emotions.

Often there are other issues and emotions affecting how you react in a situation. Think about what those could be, and how you might deal with them to reduce your anger.

7. What would be the most appropriate and effective approach of managing and controlling the situation causing unhelpful thinking or negative automatic thoughts?

You should try to think of a more constructive mechanism of dealing with the entire experience in preparation for a recurrence in future. Some of the approaches and ways of dealing with unhelpful thinking or negative automatic thoughts, and thus, symptoms of development trauma such as low self-esteem / self-criticism, anger, or distrust and insecurity are provided below.

CHAPTER 5: HOW TO COUNTER THE MALADAPTIVE BEHAVIOR OF ANGER EXTERNALIZATION

Think before speaking, and when you do ensure you calmly express your concerns. In the heat of the moment it is considerably easier to utter words that you might end up regretting later. Hence, it is advisable to take some few minutes to recollect your thoughts and think things through. You could think along the lines of: is my anger really a rational reaction to the situation or an overreaction, did the people involved really mean to wrong me or it was a honest mistake, is there a solution to the wrong the occurred.

You should also allow the other involved parties to undergo the same process, and once you have all cooled down, you can go ahead to clearly and directly express the issue that caused your frustrations while being more of assertive and less of confrontational. This implies that you can share your needs and concerns without trying to control or inflict pain on the other involved parties. Also, you should focus more on resolving the issue that made you angry other than focusing on the matter itself and why you are irate. Once you have successfully resolved the matter at hand, you are less likely to feel irritated and frustrated by the whole situation.

Besides, you should endeavor to learn and practice relaxation skills whenever you are angry. There are numerous activities you can undertake to achieve relaxation, but some of the main strategies include: performing a deep breathing exercise, repeating a certain calming phrase like "cool down", thinking of a scene of place you find to be relaxing, doing some yoga poses, or listening to music.

Last, you should involve yourself in some physical activity or body exercise. This is because psychologists have determined that physical activity tends to reduce psychological stress that often causes fits of anger. The body exercise you perform doesn't have to be extensive or intensive, as it can involve simple activity such as walking.

CHAPTER 6: HOW TO MINIMIZE THE MALADAPTIVE BEHAVIOR OF SELF-CRITICISM

An individual experiencing self-criticism as a result of development trauma can apply and utilize a type of mindfulness meditation referred to as loving-kindness meditation in order to enhance and sustain emotional wellbeing. This form of mindfulness meditation has also been proven to be fundamental in regards to transforming self-criticism into self-love. Loving-kindness meditation basically involves repetitively telling yourself phrases such as "May I be safe, may I be happy, may I be healthy, may I live with ease" is silence for about 5 minutes. A practicing psychologist has vouched for this coping mechanism by stating that most of the patients that adopt it often notice changes within a few weeks.

Besides, the issue of self-criticism can be addressed and resolved by focusing on every little win you achieve and celebrating these wins accordingly. This can be achieved through a method referred to as spot the success whereby one develops some form of a list that is the exact opposite of a to-do list, which is referred to as a done list. With this technique, you ensure that you record or write 10 actions that you successfully undertook within the day with positive or rather beneficial outcomes for you or others. The actions you record do not have to be significant or extraordinary as every small achievement such as getting out of bed, doing a favor for a friend, and going to the gym is worthy to be recorded in the done list. This practice causes the development of sense in your brain that you are actually good at doing something, which is a significant mitigating element for self-criticism.

Also, the subconscious part of our mind that often fuels self-criticism in human beings is generally a different entity from our conscious mind. While we can control how the conscious mind thinks, there is little we can do to monitor and manage our subconscious mind as it functions independently. Perceiving the thoughts from our subconscious minds as not ours, but rather a phenomenon that we get to access and witness helps us distance ourselves from the inner critic. Thus, when you experience a moment of unhelpful thinking or negative automatic thoughts that for example insinuates that you are lazy, when voicing these thoughts avoid saying that you're lazy but rather say your inner critic says you're lazy. After distancing yourself from the inner critic in your subconscious mind it becomes easier to argue against or ignore the critic rather than perceiving the criticism as a form of self-condemnation.

Last, you can set up a container similar to a "swear jar" but specifically meant for self-criticism. Hence, each time you undergo a moment of self-criticism, you put a coin into the jar. Psychologists have stated that the jar should be placed somewhere that is highly visible to you. And, as you eventually fill up the jar with coins, this will be a sign to your conscious brain that you are becoming more aware of unhelpful thinking or negative automatic thoughts, and the effect they cause on your feelings and actions. Over time, the rate at which you add coins to your self-criticism jar might reduce as compared to when you started off. Visualizing the progress of trying to increase awareness of your unhelpful thinking or negative automatic thoughts can be rewarding for your conscious mind, and thus, motivating.

CHAPTER 7: HOW TO UNDO THE MALADAPTIVE BEHAVIOR OF DISTRUST AND INSECURITY

When you have trust and insecurity issues, one of the techniques you can utilize and apply to cope with this behavioral pattern is developing trust on a slower and stable basis. For instance, rather than avoiding relationships because you are distrustful and insecure regarding other people, you could give them time to earn your trust. Case in point, if you're focused on a romantic relationship, you could for instance start off with small talk to familiarize with each other a little bit. Afterwards, you could organize for dates in public places to start engaging in personal talks about topics such as family and social background, dreams and goals, or beliefs and values. If you determine that your personalities align to some extent, you could proceed to open up about your trust and insecurity issues to determine how your partner will accommodate you. If you reach a suitable arrangement, you will find it easier to trust them onwards.

As stated above, it is very important to open up about your trust and insecurity issues when trying to develop a new relationship. You don't have to necessarily mention every little detail such the experiences you underwent to develop these issues, but talking about your struggles with trust can help others understand you better and know how to relate with you in order to avoid breaking your trust towards them. Open communication with other people can be vital in making them more aware of how their actions can impact your relationship

Moreover, if you have trust and insecurity issues, you might find that these issues are not only externalized but also internalized. This implies that you might distrust yourself just as much as you are distrustful of others. This can be exhibited by being unsure of your capability to handle important responsibilities among other cognitive patterns. Rather than avoid participating in various situations because you lack distrust towards yourself, you should occasionally take the risk and believe in yourself. Once you handle the situation effectively and successfully, you'll start trusting yourself more. You'll also start questioning your trust and insecurity issues towards other people because you'll discover that you trusted yourself and ended up not being disappointed so trusting other might have a similar outcome. You should note that trusting yourself doesn't mean never questioning yourself or your choices, being impulsive, or living a riskier life. Trusting yourself is more of developing stronger self-awareness about a distrust of yourself, which can aid you in regards to making judgement and interacting with others.

Finally, you should learn to create a distinction between the desire for trust and control. Psychologists have determined that people with trust and insecurity issues often have an underlying need to be in control of every situation they encounter. If their needs are not met, they often end up developing distrust towards other people in that situation. The mistrust can be manifested through feelings of betrayal of being taken advantage of in case you lack full and complete control of a situation. But, such behavioral patterns tend to cause hurt and pain with relationships from a long term perspective. Increased awareness of your trust and control needs enables you teach yourself to set limits regarding how much control you should aim to acquire and yield in a certain situation. This can enable you build trust more effectively with other people.

Overall, among individuals experiencing development trauma, self-criticism, anger, and distrust or insecurity tend to be the main feelings encountered. Thus, being able to control these 3 emotions can aid you control the other subsequent thoughts and emotions. For instance, self-criticism often leads to issues such as low self-esteem and regressive behavior (need for constant attention and reassurance). Thus, being able to effectively cope with self-criticism means ability to deal with low self-esteem and regressive behavior by extension. Also, being able to deal with distrust and insecurity issues implies developing the capacity to create and maintain relationships. Besides, managing to control your anger, more so from the perspective of internalization, could help address the issue of psychological dissociation or zoning out, and thus, resolve the challenge of troubled learning.

ABOUT THE AUTHOR

Zecaina N.

Is a firm believer in the concept of patient-centred healthcare and has therefore made it his life mission to empower individuals struggling with various medical complications through provision of healthcare knowledge. With this mission, he hopes to help people recover from their conditions in a cost-effective, home-based, and efficient manner.

BOOKS BY THIS AUTHOR

Fighting Depressive Illness And Suicidal Thoughts: First-Hand Experience Of Treating And Healing From Depression

The Obesity Textbook Of How Lose Weight Like Crazy - A Weight Loss Memoir With A Guideline To Cut Fat And Shed Weight Fast

Women Reproductive Health: Endometriosis,

Pcos, Ovarian Cysts, Uterine Fibroids, Dysmenorrhea, And Amenorrhea Treatment - The Hormone Repair Manual